At Bat III

Poems About Baseball and Other Sports

At Bat III

Poems About Baseball and Other Sports by

Mel Glenn

© 2025 Mel Glenn. All rights reserved.
This material may not be reproduced in any form, published,
reprinted, recorded, performed, broadcast,
rewritten, or redistributed without
the explicit permission of Mel Glenn.
All such actions are strictly prohibited by law.

Cover design by Shay Culligan
Cover image by Adam Vilimek

ISBN: 978-1-63980-771-0

Kelsay Books
502 South 1040 East, A-119
American Fork, Utah 84003
Kelsaybooks.com

*for Sam, a good, true friend and eagle-eyed editor, with thanks
and Mark, also a gifted editor, who has allowed me to explore the
world of baseball through his site, baseballbard.com*

Contents

1. Batter Up! (Baseball Poems)

A Boy Grows in Brooklyn	13
A Baseball/Poetry Link	14
A Baseball Manifesto	15
A Good Nap Ruined	16
"And Now a Word From . . ."	17
A Letter to the Baseball Gods	18
Angling for a Poem	19
Bang the Drum Slowly	20
Baseball and Language	21
Box Score	22
Brooklyn Bridge	23
Caught in the Middle	24
Defensive Indifference	25
Designated Hitter	26
Fingers Crossed	27
First Place	28
Ghosts of Brooklyn Past	29
Grapefruit League II	30
How Ya Gonna Keep 'Em?	31
I Can Hit Better Than That	32
I Coulda Been a Sportswriter	33
In Praise of the Lowly Bunt	34
It's a Looooooong Season	35
Ivan Delinov	36
Jackson Pollock Paints Baseball	37
Kevin Costner and Me	38
Marianne Moore: Poet, Baseball Fan	39
My Son, the Ballplayer	40

Namby-Pambies	41
Nicknames	42
Patchwork	43
Pinch Hitters	44
Promises, Promises	45
Radio Days II	46
Rain Delay	47
Robots Keep Out!	48
Sam Diamond, Sports Fan	49
Sam's Memories	50
Screaming into the Set	51
Sent Up, Sent Down	52
Signage	53
Spring Training Acrostic	54
Starting Pitching	55
The Injury Bug	56
The Last Out	57
The Old Ballplayer in Love	58
The Phenom	59
The Playing Field	60
The Play's the Thing	61
The Rook	62
The Visiting Psychologist	63
Trading Places	64
We Were the Generals	65
When Nelson Takes the Mound	66
When Baseball Players Were Tough	67
Who Remembers Herb Score?	68
Why We Are Fans	69
You Take It Too Personally	70

2. Poems About Other Sports

There's More to Life Than Baseball	73
Winter of My Discontent	74
Racing For Life	75
A George Carlin Basketball Poem	76
Air Jordan	77
In the Dark	78
D.J. Tucker	79
Darius Mills	80
Joel's Father	81
An Homage to John Updike	82
The Mountaineer	83
Annie Roberts	84
Martin Andrews	85
A $600,000 Sack?	86
A Father and His Son	87
Arco, Idaho	88
On Thin Ice	89
Amanda Berne	90
Penny Coles	91
Juliette	92
Dark Tennis	93
The Underdog	94

1. Batter Up!
(Baseball Poems)

A Boy Grows in Brooklyn

Growing up in Brooklyn
gave you a passport to sports.
There was the playground, the corner, the stoop,
all providing the venue for your emerging athletic skills.
We had all manner of balls to shoot, hit, and punch.
Liberated from school, you flocked with your friends
for pick-up games that lasted far into the evening.
You learned teamwork, the value of friendship,
and how to handle victory and defeat.

As you grew older participation
gave way to spectating.
You followed different teams with ardor.
You invested your non-work energy
into rooting for your favorites,
exulting in their successes,
while despairing in their failures.

Yes, baseball is and was my primary love.
It drives me to root for my teams
and inspires me to write my poetry.
But the rich panoply of all sports
gives us hope, providing meaning
to our mundane lives.
We wake up thinking about the next contest,
living vicariously through those
lucky enough to still play kids' games,
while recalling our own successes
on our childhood fields of play.

A Baseball/Poetry Link

When my team is playing good ball,
words flow from my pen
as clean as a line single to right.
My metaphors take flight and fall
in the reader's lap out in the bleachers.
Inspiration comes to me,
as brilliant as a manager's hunch
to go with the hit and run.
But when my team has lost five in a row,
my words seem frozen in the batter's box,
much like a batter fooled by a called third strike.
My metaphors never bounce past the pitcher's mound,
and my similes prompt the crowd
to roundly boo my creative efforts.
Inspiration fails me,
as deflating as a final 11–0 drubbing.
So, Mr. Manager, get your team to do better.
Then maybe my literary work will be a hit.

A Baseball Manifesto

The Cincinnati Reds have issued
the following proclamation:

"Baseball players, come join us.
You have nothing to lose but your bats.
Rise up from the lumpenproletariat,
cast off the shackles placed upon you
by heartless managers and commissioners.
Create a new baseball order
in which all players will be equally treated.
No more fights over money.
No more contracts tying you
to one specific geographical area.
Every player, regardless of position,
will be treated with respect,
all in the service of a greater good:
To wave a championship banner
in the May Day parade.
Listen to our Five-Year Plan.
Come to our training sessions in the spring.
We will once more make baseball
the opium of the masses."

A Good Nap Ruined

I listen to my team on the radio these days,
keeping the volume at a level
just below active involvement.
Like the ocean, the noise of batters and fielders
dips and rises in succeeding waves.
I wait for the crest of applause,
when a home run is struck, or a fielder
makes a play he wasn't expected to make.
Sometimes, if the action is particularly slow,
I fall into a light sleep, knowing
that if any dramatic point were to arise,
my ears would catch the increased commotion.
Then, my brain would quickly imagine the action.
In this manner I maintain my loyalty to my team,
while affording myself time and place
to attend to more immediate concerns.
There will always be matters requiring my attention,
but I am secure in the knowledge
I can always get back to what is
of paramount importance—the ebb and flow
of the tides of the game.

"And Now a Word From . . ."

"Good afternoon from . . .
ServPro: Like it never even happened
. . . Citi Field, where today . . .
by your Tri-Honda dealers
. . . we are bringing you . . .
Bigelow Tea: In A TeaProudly way
. . . the third game of a . . .
Peerless boilers are the best boilers
. . . series between the . . .
Fireworks, presented by Goya
. . . Pittsburgh Pirates and . . .
Key Food, your key to savings
. . . your New York Mets.
Dial Oil Heat, keeping you warm!
Starting pitchers and lineups . . .
Injury.com has you covered
. . . after these few words."
*Barnabas Hospital: Let's be
healthy together!*

A Letter to the Baseball Gods

Dear Sirs,

You're kiddin' me, right?
Just when I think my team
is headed for its best season in years,
you pull the rug out from under me,
and strike down our best ballplayer
with a pulled hamstring.
Do you enjoy torturing me?
Do you take particular pleasure
in making me totally miserable?
True, there are 25 other guys on the team,
but he is the one whose batting average
I follow in the box score every day.
I know you sirs are quite busy,
directing the bounce of the ball,
the arc of the pitch, but c'mon,
let me have a break here.
Allow me, please, my small hopes
to get me through my rather ordinary life.

Sincerely yours,
A Most Dispirited Fan

Angling for a Poem

The old man, sometimes a poet,
and wearing his worn baseball cap,
was angling for a baseball poem,
something that would show
his love of the sport.
Such poems, he thought,
live under the sea,
traveling in different schools,
swimming at various depths.
Some longer, larger poems
troll the murky bottom, unseen
by poets searching for them.
Others, the smaller, lighter ones
are easy to pull in with
a few light flicks of his poised pen.
He, poor angler, seemingly
working for scale pay,
cast out his lines
in the hopes of landing
a big catch, a poem rich in
baseball metaphors.
I need a bigger boat, he thought,
a larger craft fully rigged
to reel in the bigger haul
from the wellspring
of my imagination.
"I am tired of just skimming
the surface of my talents,"
he said to himself.
"I need to explore the
currents in my brain to capture
the largest baseball poem I possibly can."
We wish the old man good luck.

Bang the Drum Slowly

Few people have heard
of John Adams, but for
the people of Cleveland,
he is the ultimate fan.
For over 3,700 games,
starting in 1973, he
would carry his big bass drum,
sit in the bleachers, and
bang out a booming beat
with a mallet in each hand.
In an age when million-dollar athletes
want even more, how refreshing
to hear of a man so loyal and devoted.
How admirable to meet a fan
following his passion, rooting
for the home team, even if that team
was terrible, as the Indians (now Guardians) were.
The Bradys and the Irvings of the
sports world should heed the example
of this simple man with his simple fervor.
John Adams died this week.
Not many will remember his name,
least of all the money-hungry athletes
we mistakenly put on pedestals,
hanging on their every word.

Baseball and Language

So ingrained in American culture,
we don't realize how baseball and language
are inextricably linked, with baseball phrases
a part of our everyday conversation.

To wit:
"Right, left, center"
(not a political label).
"Hit and run"
(an unfortunate, criminal accident).
"A single"
(someone alone on a Saturday night).
"Sacrifice"
(what mothers do for their children every day).
"Out at home"
(a divorce).
"The wind-up"
(the end of a romance).
"Batter up"
(cake preparations).
"Designated hitter"
(a contract killer).
"Relief pitcher"
(beer at the end of a work day).
"Pop-up"
(a fun children's book).
"Starting rotation"
(laundry machine turned on).

So, the next time you're at a game,
notice how you are playing with words.

Box Score

When I was a kid,
I poured over the box score
to see how my favorite players were doing.
What was Gil Hodges batting,
and how many putouts did Duke Snider make?
The box scores improved my math skills.
I learned how to calculate
batting averages and earned run averages.
I knew that two for five was .400 for the day,
a pretty good result for my new favorite rookie.
Wouldn't it be nice if we could all get
daily report cards like that?
How many meetings did you average last week?
What was your average commuting time last month?
I don't know if I am up for such daily scrutiny,
but I would like my successes and failures
recorded in the paper for all time.
Do kids today even bother looking at a box score,
let alone studying its magical intricacies?
I doubt it. They're too busy
playing Candy Crush on their iPhone.
And let's not even talk about keeping a score card.

Brooklyn Bridge

This is less a paean
to the iconic bridge
which opened in 1883
and was at that time the
longest suspension bridge ever.
But rather this is more of a
bridge to my Brooklyn childhood
where I fell in love
with the ballet of baseball.
I played on sandlots, in playgrounds,
anywhere I could swing my stickball bat
and catch the ubiquitous "Spaldeen."
The Dodgers deserted me,
but I still have minor-league ball
played in Coney Island by the boardwalk,
where I go with my friend, Sam,
a fellow baseball aficionado.
It is no accident that
Brooklyn and Baseball begin with the
same capital letter, so when I see
my Cyclones (named for the famous
roller coaster, a few blocks
beyond the left field wall),
that Brooklyn Baseball bridge takes me back
to the good times of my childhood,
where I am once again safe at home.

Caught in the Middle

I am lucky enough to have
friends on either side
of the religious diamond,
fundamentalists who swing from the right,
and atheists who bat from the left.
I stand squarely in the middle,
unsure which side to root for,
let alone play for.
I am caught between
piety and protest, tradition and rebellion.
There are so many teams,
as there are so many religions.
For which team do I sign a long-term
contract on the dotted line?
The Pittsburgh Protestants?
The Boston Buddhists?
The Miami Muslims,
or the Jersey City Jews?
Doesn't God pitch for all the teams?
Who is to say which team is best,
which team is strongest,
which team leads the league?
We are all essentially on the same playing field.
We are all part of the same cosmic lineup.
We need to feel connected,
no matter which team we play for.
We do not wish to be wandering alone,
unattached, in the far reaches of the outfield.

Defensive Indifference

What is up with that?
It is indeed a slippery slope
when you no longer care what the runner does.
It is a short step to hell to refuse to try and nab him,
even if the score is decidedly in your favor.
What if other professions were equally indifferent?
The surgeon who does not stitch properly
because the operation is too easy.
The teacher who does not adequately prepare
because the students are too smart.
The prosecutor who does not try his case
because the man before the bar is patently guilty.
The builder who installs shoddy materials
because he can get away with it.
No, no, baseball provides our moral code.
There are universal truths and time-honored regulations,
laws, if you will, that are to be followed.
If we don't do what we are supposed to do,
chaos is loosed, and anarchy ensues.
Therefore, we can't possibly have indifference,
defensive or otherwise, in baseball or in life.

Designated Hitter

I need a designated hitter
to step in for me
to handle tasks I can't,
like taxes, and arguments
with my younger brother.
I need a designated hitter
to go shopping for me
when I can't seem
to lift myself out of bed.
I need a designated hitter
who helps me with the
new technology that is way
past my comprehension.
I need a designated hitter
to find new friends for me,
a new group with whom
I can compare aches and pains,
and not feel like a constant complainer,
or see me as some aging senior citizen.
Designated hitters shouldn't be reserved
just for ballplayers who are young anyway.
They are needed for old codgers like me.

Fingers Crossed

Historically, a sign to invoke
the power of the cross,
a concentration of good wishes
for a desired outcome.
Maybe I should cross my toes, too
for the outlook isn't brilliant
for my team this year.
How do you hope and pray
for a winning season
when you know your team
did not do enough in the off-season
to attract a quality staff?
You live on a river of hope,
on a raft that carries your
dreams to a winning port of call.
On your raft fit the hopes of
your city and of the players
you have followed for years.
Your raft may capsize, leaving
you no chance to make the playoffs,
but for now, at the headwaters
of the season you try to envision
only smooth sailing ahead.

First Place

First place in August!
You've got to be kidding me.
But there it is!
As obvious as a shiny new penny
you find on the sidewalk.
All things are possible now!
A new job, a new love,
a spring in your step
as you quickly pass by pedestrians
on a busy Brooklyn street.
The world takes on a new hue;
colors are brighter, food tastes better.
And at the game,
you join with the community of fans
who believe this late in the season
that playoffs are definitely part of your future.
So, may the beat go on.
May home runs sail into the right field bleachers.
The world is a baseball game,
and you stand on top of it, in first place.

Ghosts of Brooklyn Past

Hey, Peewee!
Hello, Duke!
Good to see you, Gil!
You've been away a long, long time,
but now it's time to don your uniforms again,
and take your seats at the Barclays Center,
the new home of the Brooklyn Nets.
Campy, Robinson, I didn't forget you guys.
You can join in on the 4th quarter chants of
"Brooklyn, Brooklyn."
Better yet, move your ephemeral selves to mid-court,
and stand in the batter's box pantheon
of my childhood heroes, past, present, and future.
Other witnesses will soon share in the celebration.
Whitman will write a poem, Mailer, a novel,
and fireworks will light up the Coney Island sky.
The sports emptiness of 55 years
(when you guys left for the West Coast)
will be filled by raucous, cheering fans.
You can go home again, especially
if there is a bright, new reason
for exchanging cleats for sneakers.

Grapefruit League II

"Hope is a thing with feathers,"
Emily Dickinson famously said.
I try to remember that
as I scan the box scores
of spring training games,
wondering if each player
I don't recognize will
blossom into an all-star player.
Hope is a batter stepping up to the plate,
a pitcher beginning his wind-up,
a manager filling out his line-up card.
Hope is the next batter,
the next game, the next series.
It is the tenuous string to the heart
that keeps one alive.
It is the smile of a young kid
pounding his glove, praying
that the next ground ball
will be hit to him so he can make the play.
Hope is as large as a grapefruit
which maybe will not become pulverized
as the season slips into summer.

How Ya Gonna Keep 'Em?

How ya gonna keep 'em
down on the farm
when they are blowing up Triple-A?
All spring training I followed
my four favorite rookies
as they made their bids
to become major leaguers.
They all had outstanding springs,
so how do the powers-that-be
decide who goes up and
who goes down?
Do age, contracts and seniority
supersede new, raw talent?
Veterans are there for a reason,
but what do you do with
the exciting talent bubbling below?
When is it decided that
"the torch is passed to a new generation"?
I am glad I am not the gatekeeper
who has to make such decisions,
though I long to see my rookies move up.

I Can Hit Better Than That

When my team is in the throes
of a bottomless batting slump,
I can hit better than that.
When the pitchers for my team
refuse to find the strike zone,
I can throw better than that.
When the infielders for my team
treat grounders like coffee too hot to handle,
I can catch better than that.
When the outfielders for my team
look to *other* fielders to snag the routine fly,
I can track the ball better than that.
They can't be that bad, that awful, can they?
It's painful to a watch a ship slowly sinking
below the .500 water line, glub, glub.
So, stir your spirits, men, wake up those bats.
Add adhesive to your fielding mitts.
Know and have pity that I can't possibly endure
one more losing season of futility and despair.
Send me in, coach. I can't be any worse
than the team you are putting out there daily.

I Coulda Been a Sportswriter

I coulda been a sportswriter,
handling all sports with clichés and aplomb.
I coulda followed all the athletes,
and caught their monosyllables
with my little tape recorder.
"How'd you pitch today?"
"I felt my fastball was working."
"But you got knocked out in the 3rd."
"Can't win 'em all. Tomorrow is another day."
I coulda been a sportswriter,
with a minor in business.
"So, what do you think of your contract negotiations?"
"I ain't gettin' enough."
"They're offering you 4 million over 5 years."
"I'm worth more than that."
Instead I traded my typewriter for chalk,
and fielded questions like:
"Who wrote 'The Diary of Anne Frank'?"
"Is the opposite of 'dilate' dying early?"
I coulda been many things,
but chose, as it turns out,
the road most traveled by.

In Praise of the Lowly Bunt

Oh, ye of little distance,
the favored stroke of players and pitchers
mired below the Mendoza line,
square up your shoulders,
and your bat, stand with pride
that your dribble down the line
weighs more important than
a towering fly ball out.
What greater call than to sacrifice,
to lay down your life to advance the runner?
You may never be heralded
on the evening sports broadcasts,
nor achieve acclaim within
the halls of Cooperstown.
But true aficionados of the game know
the importance of your achievements
has little to do with length.
So, continue your shortened travels
along the infield grass, confident
it is not necessarily a bad thing
to come up a little bit short.

It's a Looooooong Season

My friend, Sam, tells me
I have no patience
when it comes to baseball.
He's right.
At the end of the first month
I am disconsolate that my team
is playing lackluster baseball.
"Bring up the rookies," I cry,
(who are tearing up Triple-A.)
"Get rid of the manager."
But patience is required here.
To wit: a little research reveals—
1917, the Boston Braves, 15 games
out in July, won the pennant.
1978, the New York Yankees, 14 games
out in July, won the pennant.
1993, the Atlanta Braves, 10 games
out in July, won the pennant.
I really must get a grip.
It's a loooong season.

Ivan Delinov

Oh, yes, I am looking for summer job, new one.
Do you have opportunity for me?
Last summer I work at ballpark
selling beer, pretzels and peanuts.
It was nice to be in fresh air,
but I am looking for new, how you say,
higher level of celery.
Oh, yes, salary, thank you.
Ah, America is fine country.
Such big difference between
throwing pretzels and throwing fastballs.
It bothered me that star players
earn salary of $1,000,000 a year,
which is about $143,000 a month
for seven months' work,
which is about $36,000 a week,
which is about $5,000 a day,
while I worked for peanuts.

Jackson Pollock Paints Baseball

In his studio, when the weather warms,
Jackson Pollock thinks of the colors
he needs to present a portrait
of the coming baseball season.
He lines up his cans of paint,
puts his large canvas on the floor
and drips his paint all over it
to capture the tapestry of spring training.
Two primary colors dominate:
The expansive blue of the sky,
and the forest green of the outfield.
Other colors are sprinkled in:
The fire-engine red of a Cardinal's uniform,
the liquid orange of a Mets' baseball cap.
Still more colors are dripped in:
the white of resin bags and baseballs,
the tan and black of baseball bats.
Take these colors, Jackson,
mix them all together
and you have prepared
the backdrop of baseball.
Sounds will come on Opening Day,
but the picture you have completed
will last in our mind's eye all through
the spring, summer and fall.

Kevin Costner and Me

On the evening of
the annual "Field of Dreams" game,
I always tear up when I remember
Kevin Costner asking in the film,
"Hey, Dad, you wanna have a catch?"
My father, European by birth,
had a hard time understanding
American culture, much less
American sports, preferring instead
to devote his leisure time
to writing and study.
I discovered basketball and football
on my own, but they were
poor substitutes for a relationship
cemented by baseball.
I am still Kevin Costner looking to play catch.
My father never played catch with me.
My father never played catch with me.

Marianne Moore: Poet, Baseball Fan

Oh, Marianne, you used to go
to the Dodger games, right?
The old Brooklyn Dodgers,
who played in the small confines
of Ebbets Field in the '50s.
I might have seen you there,
and together we might have written
a poem or two together
showing our love for Dodger blue.
Reese, Campy, the Duke, and Hodges
were the stuff of my childhood dreams
that one day I would take the relay
from Furillo and cut down the runner
trying to score from first on a double.
By the end of the game we both
would have finished our verses;
then we would break for refreshments
while extolling the praises of our Bums.
No more waiting until next year.
Time for poetry then and now.

My Son, the Ballplayer

"You're asking me about my little Joshy?
Of course, he never plays on Friday nights
or Saturday afternoons. (It's in his contract.)
And, for sure, like Koufax, he would never
suit up for the World Series in October,
at least not if the game was on the High Holy Days
(should the team be so fortunate).
Between innings, he can be seen reading
a real book, not a playbook.
But would it kill him to call me, his mother?
He has the money.
I constantly worry about him,
afraid that some shiksa goddess
will ensnare him, even though he's 28,
a boy still, playing a boy's game.
He has his kosher food delivered to him.
As a good mother, I send him rugelach.
His teammates love my brisket.
When he strikes out, I can
almost hear him say, 'Oy,' but when
he hits a home run, I can see him exult
with a cry of 'Halevi' as he circles the bases.
He proudly wears #18 (chai), and has told me
he is grateful, the little pisher,
to play with chutzpah the Great American Game.
I'm so proud of him, I'm kvelling."

Namby-Pambies

Where are the pitchers of yesteryear,
the Seavers and the Spahns,
the Marichals and the Martinezes,
the Ryans and the Reynolds?
Those pitchers were expected
to go the full nine innings,
and usually did just that.
Now, a "quality" start
consists of five innings.
Now, relief pitchers
are regularly slated to start a game.
Yes, pitchers throw harder these days.
Yes, spin rates are ever faster,
prompting an elevator ride
of pitchers sent down
to the minor leagues
for rehab starts because their arms were hurt,
while fresh limbs are called up as needed.
(I blame the pitch clock.)
Pitchers are not what they used to be,
but then again, neither am I.
Perhaps we're all namby-pambies now.

Nicknames

Having been tagged with the nickname
"the Professor" ever since I was little,
I am charmed by the names given
to the glorious heroes of the past,

Reggie Jackson, "Mr. October"
What happened to the other months?
"Shoeless Joe" Jackson
Could you play without cleats?
Stan "the Man" Musial
What else could you be? A girl?
Ted Williams, "the Splendid Splinter"
Does it hurt?
Lou Gehrig, "the Iron Horse"
Hard to move around the base?
Dennis "Oil Can" Boyd
Do you need help for your pitching arm?
Harold "Pie" Traynor
Do you eat while in the field?
Jim "Catfish" Hunter
You'd rather go fishing, right?
Walter "Big Train" Johnson
Ready for the team's road trip?
Edwin "Preacher" Roe, Sal "the Barber" Maglie
Did you consider other professions?

There are hundreds more,
some flattering, some not.
I think I'll stick with mine.

Patchwork

The New York Yankees' uniform,
pristine and pin-striped,
with nary a player's name
printed on the back has now been
besmirched by corporate greed
with the appearance of an
insurance logo on the left sleeve.
The Yankees (worth $7.1 billion, says Forbes)
will get $25 million annually,
succumbing to the dubious distinction
that they need even more money.
What's next? Will their uniforms
be covered with more and more logos
for everything from diaper swabs,
to energy drinks, to motor oil?
Will players patrol the outfield
emblazoned like race car drivers,
who have become walking billboards?
Baseball jerseys are quite naturally
stained with dirt in the course of a game.
Must we sully them even more with ads?

Pinch Hitters

At New York's Citi Field,
if Salinger catches, Who's on First?
Where have you gone, Joe DiMaggio, center field?
O'Reilly plays a very right field,
and Stewart patrols in left.
King George guards the line at third,
and Jesus is due for the Second Coming.
It's indeed a short stop from Queens to Brooklyn.
And on the mound, the big right-hander, God
throws us a variety of curves,
designed to baffle us mere mortals.
We strike out more often than not,
with our batting averages way below .300.
But on some sunlit days,
or some moonlit nights,
we step up to the plate,
defy the odds, and deliver the walk-off hit,
making us temporary winners
before the game is ultimately called.

Promises, Promises

The reason we adore baseball,
the reason we hold onto our boyhood dreams,
is that the game provides us with something
often lacking in our humdrum lives:
HOPE!
"Our pitching will be stronger next year."
"We will be a different team."
"We are going to be in the mix in October."
To change sports metaphors,
we surf on the crest of promises,
which sustains us through
the long winter night.
Our lives may lack a future.
We may tremble in our insecurities,
but if the carrot stick of
future diamond glory is offered,
"wait 'til next year,"
we grab at it, hungrily.
We will no longer have to
wait 'til next year,
because promises prove
next year is already here.

Radio Days II

It is a constant theme
that the world far outstrips me,
moving at such astonishing speed
that it leaves me thrashing
helplessly in the dust.
But every so often I collect
my breath by turning on the
old-fashioned AM radio.
Right now, the '50s comfort
of the Mets' radio broadcast
from faraway Oakland, California,
puts me back in the last century
when I used to fall asleep
with the soft buzz of
the game in my ear.
Our lives were not eaten up by
the hungry demands of technology.
I am a 21st century Luddite
who would like to be left alone
with his radio, so I may once more
live in the past and not the present.
Even the commercials then were soothing.

Rain Delay

Rain delay,
life on hold,
pleasure postponed,
I'm sitting in the stands,
under an umbrella,
wondering if the game will be called.
The tarp blankets the infield,
and I wonder what to do with myself.
Get a hot dog,
find my soul,
maybe a beer, too,
plan my retirement,
go for a walk around the stadium,
contemplate the meaning of life.
Maybe if the rain's not too bad,
ballplayers could wear those
little umbrellas attached to their caps.
But it's important not to be impatient,
to just sit back and take in the view,
to see the beauty of it and
realize how lucky I am to enjoy
the quiet of this afternoon with the
pitter-pattering of the rain all around me.

Robots Keep Out!

As an experiment, several teams
in lower Class A Minor League ball
will use robot umpires behind the plate
called the "Automatic Ball/Strike System."
It's the beginning of the end
of baseball as we know it.
It's like dancing without music,
theater without actors,
peanut butter without jelly.
It's totally unacceptable.
In the age of tech,
have we become less than human?
Ballplayers will be deprived of the
opportunity to yell at the umpire.
Managers will be unable
to kick dirt over the plate.
What then will be next "advancement"?
Automaton pitchers throwing to
automaton batters with creaking machinery?
We might as well cancel the season
and turn major league baseball into
some kind of futuristic video game.

Sam Diamond, Sports Fan

In the midst of the pandemic,
with all the sports arenas closed,
I miss the crack of the bat,
the slap of a hockey stick,
the whoosh of the net,
the thud of a tackle.
I miss that part of my life.
I do not want
a half of a season,
a third of a season,
or a quarter of a season.
I want a full season,
where I can watch my teams
fall and climb in the standings,
where play regularly occurs
over a full schedule,
and where players have time
to grow and develop.
Now I am playing with half a deck,
a third of my interest,
a quarter of my enthusiasm.
Sports are a missing part of my life,
and I feel that part of me amputated.

Sam's Memories

My friend Sam lost his father
when he was only nine.
He cherished the memories
of watching ball games together on the couch
in front of the wood-paneled Zenith TV,
the seven-year-old's head
resting on his dad's lap.
Strange for Brooklyn,
his father was a New York Giants fan;
stranger still, sticking with them
when they left for California.
So naturally Sam inherited the team, too.

Sam and his father thought
Willie Mays was the best ballplayer ever,
so when Willie died this week,
Sam took out his old San Francisco Giants hat
and wore it proudly for days,
the tribute as much for his father
as it was for Willie,
the memories of sitting
together on the couch
fixed in his mind forever,
held as tightly as Willie catching
a long fly ball to center field.

Screaming into the Set

In the World Series
everything plays at heightened pitch,
each swing, each batter, each run,
tensions rising as innings quickly move along.
Heroes are lauded, goats vilified,
and I don't care about any of it.
Stadiums roar, announcers go bananas
as the ball sails over the right field wall.
I couldn't care less.
Strange batters, strange pitchers fill lineup cards.
I have never been to their strange cities,
even if I could accumulate the airfare.
But I remember, now over the span of 30 years,
when my home team, my team (!)
played in the Fall Classic.
I could not afford a seat in the stadium then,
so I sat glued to the TV set,
and when, after hanging on every pitch,
the last batter struck out,
I screamed with joy into the set.
But that was long ago when I was young.
Yet, I remember, I do remember.

Sent Up, Sent Down

Baseball is an adult version
of the kid's game
Chutes and Ladders.
We cheer for the Triple-A player
who has climbed the highest rung
and is told by the manager
he has made the Opening Day roster.
We feel for his teammate
who has not met expectations
and is told by the manager
he will be sent down for
more seasoning and playing time.
And we have compassion for
the highly touted pitcher who
was a lock for the starting rotation
and now suffers an inflamed elbow
and must be shut down for six weeks.
We love baseball because
it mirrors our own challenges,
the climbing and the falling,
the chasing of the dream,
no matter what the dream may be.
It is the saga of American life
where a few will rise to the top
while the rest of us will slip back
to the splendid commonplace
of everyday, ordinary life.

Signage

Something must be askew
with my fashion sense,
(if I ever had one)
that I feel I must literally
wear my sports affiliations on my sleeve.
I proudly stroll about in T-shirts and caps
emblazoned with a favorite team's logo.
Even at a minor league game,
such as the Cyclones in Coney Island,
I dutifully festoon myself with a regulation shirt
as if I am a member of the squad.
I figure it's my need to belong
to some place, organization, or community.
Or is it my need to stand out,
that I am not anonymous,
but part of something bigger than myself?
So tell me that mine is
a particularly cute cap or T-shirt,
or salute me with a knowing nod
from a fellow fan,
and I will feel like I belong for the
length of a nine-inning game and beyond.

Spring Training Acrostic

S o few phrases
P ermit the soul to
R ise to cerulean skies.
I n the Florida and Arizona sun
N eophytes attempt to impress
G rizzled old coaches with dazzling skills.
T rumpets herald the first pitch.
R ight handers deal from 60 feet away,
A nd on fields around the complex,
I nfielders, outfielders, pitchers and catchers
N ervelessly ask their bodies to
I mitate the exploits of childhood heroes.
N owhere on earth is a better promise made,
G uaranteed to reset the world on its proper orbit.

Starting Pitching

Sitting cozily by the hot stove,
I start to think about starting pitching
which ain't what it used to be.
(But then again, neither am I.)
Where are the giants (small "g")
of yesteryear who feared no batter?
Here are some hallowed recent names, like:
Gooden, Guidry, Hershiser and Valenzuela,
Maddox, Glavine, Smoltz and Rogers,
and my personal favorite, Sandy Koufax.
Or go back further in time:
Cleveland, Dean, Grove and Mathewson,
Page, Roberts, Wynn and Young,
men who would go nine innings,
without blinking, not the wimps of today
who if they go six are feted like all-stars.
Now, if a pitcher gets a boo-boo on
his hand, he is immediately taken out.
Mordecai Brown pitched with three fingers,
and Cy Young pitched over 7,000 innings.
Give me pitchers who can go the distance,
forsaking namby-pamby relief efforts,
men who will say to the manager at the mound,
"Leave me in, chief; I can strike this guy out."

The Injury Bug

Baseball players are afraid of nothin'.
They are big, powerful men
who can grip a baseball whole
with their outsized hands.
Only one small creature
can terrify championship teams,
one small varmint who
can attack an arm or a leg.
It is the Injury Bug,
the little devil who can emerge
from the infield dirt, and without
rhyme or reason, devastate
a team's post-season aspirations.
He might tighten an arm,
swell a knee, bruise a rib.
The Injury Bug laughs at
coaches and strength conditioners,
indeed anyone trying to safeguard
the players and owners' investment.
Put forth your best team, folks,
but note, the Injury Bug is lurking,
lurking, ready to strike at any moment.

The Last Out

There is a rhythm to the rain,
a pattern to the seasons.
Beginnings require completions,
and when the last ball was struck
(this time a slow grounder to third,
and a quick throw to first),
we have come full circle once more.
We're relieved at the cessation of tension,
jubilant if our favorite team has won.
Much of life defies expectation;
unforeseen events shake us all,
and uncertainties tax our emotional well-being.
We need the comfort of baseball,
the thwack of the ball into the catcher's glove,
the never varying distance between
the pitcher's mound and home plate,
the familiarity of the umpire's strike call.
So, when the last out is recorded,
we will collectively breathe a sigh of relief,
secure that the constancy of baseball
will be there again next spring,
awaiting our appeal for cosmic order.

The Old Ballplayer in Love

She was winsome,
sitting there in the faded hotel lobby
of some forgettable Triple-A city,
quite young, and very smartly dressed,
tapping delicately on her laptop,
as if there were an important conference
to attend at the local Chamber of Commerce.
She was a major-league beauty,
while he languished without distinction
in the rough-hewn minors of constant bus rides
and fast food restaurants open all night.
But even if he were a major leaguer,
she would remain out of his league,
the difference in years dealing
a death blow to any approach.
He was not so old as to ignore
the curve of her legs,
the swell of her breasts.
He continued to look, stare even,
ruing the number of past birthdays.
She was stunning, no doubt.
Yet just like with baseball games,
you win some, you lose some, he shrugged.

The Phenom

Every spring, in every camp,
there is always the Phenom,
one obscure minor leaguer
who, in the warm sun,
takes off for new heights.
He has hit three home runs
in seven plate appearances,
and the reporters covering are quick
to call him the next big thing.
Like a rocket, will he
continue to soar, hit his target
of making the major league club,
or will he flame out, fall back
into the obscurity of the minors
and the smaller American cities?
Hopes of family and friends
ride on every pitch he sees,
and only the Baseball Gods
know what his fate will be.
For the moment, though,
the decision of going up
or going down seems to hang
in the air, like a high fly to right.

The Playing Field

When striking out regularly
in Little League ball,
I repaired to my room
and entered the realm
of my fantasy baseball league.
Before computers, all I needed was
a pair of dice, spiral notebooks,
and my imagination to call to life
the United Baseball Association.
There were eight teams, two divisions
located in real cities across the land,
even a world series at season's end.
If I couldn't be a ballplayer
I could sound like one doing
my own play-by-play broadcasts.
Those games played in the UBA
created the bridge from my childhood
to the playing fields of adolescence.
Somewhere in my closet
the old notebooks gather dust.

The Play's the Thing

My mother has always stood
in the theater wings of my life,
pushing me on stage or onto the field
before I was ready to perform or play.
She has always been the one
to encourage me to try for different things.
"Of course, you should try out
for the school softball team.
Of course, you should try out
for the lead in the school play.
I was the starting shortstop for the team, you know.
I was the female lead for the play, you know."
Of course, I know, given her monologues,
presented center stage for my instruction.
"I lettered in three sports, you know," she says.
Of course, I know; she has cued my lines
to the point where I don't control my own voice.
I am the understudy to her life.
She upstages me all the time in front of my friends.
She doesn't act her age—she acts mine!
I fear she will always seek the bright lights,
pushing me further into the background and off the field.

The Rook

With the race long over,
with my team mired in last place,
the September call-ups breathe
new life into a moribund season,
There he stands, the Rook,
just called up from Triple-A
awaiting the first pitch of
his major league career.
He eschews a ball low and away,
and then, crack, he scorches
a line drive over the
right fielder's head.
The crowd erupts in a standing ovation,
a brief moment of hope in an
errant season, a harbinger?
The ball is tossed into the dugout,
a gift for his parents to treasure.
And for one shining moment, this season,
if not the next one, beams electric.

The Visiting Psychologist

After being shut out three times in a row,
team owners called in a visiting psychologist
who offered the following analysis:
"Your continuous failure to reach home
suggests a profound childhood trauma,
one where your non-sports parents
refused to play catch with you, favoring
an older brother who became a doctor.
You acted out by flailing with your stick,
all to no avail, the glare of lights at night
blinding you to sibling rivalry.
You made too many errors while
standing on the playing field of life.
You crashed into walls, mindlessly,
and blew the opportunity to save yourself.
Realize you are fated to fail
70% of the time and accept it.
Nevertheless, swing for the fences,
forget all your internal turmoil.
This will go a long way towards
improving your stats at home."

Trading Places

Oh, the life of a baseball card,
to be summarily flipped and traded
on the sidewalks of Brooklyn.
I remember the high drama
of cards won and lost when I was kid,
when afternoons turned bright or dark
depending on whether my card
was closest to the wall, the action
as mercurial as stocks rising and falling.
How do real ballplayers similarly adjust
to the possibility of a sudden trade,
a sudden change of fortunes?
Do they count their blessings
if traded to a better team?
Do they cry over their misfortune
if dealt to a cellar-dweller?
I wonder if baseball players
are as fragile as my old collection of
bubble-gum cards wrapped in rubber bands
as they get tossed into the trade winds of life.

We Were the Generals

We were the Generals,
a little league before there was a Little League,
sandlot ball on real sandlots.
No uniforms, but crayon-scrawled
names written on white tee shirts
with "Generals" emblazoned
along with your favorite number,
(mine was number 4, in honor of
the Duke of Flatbush, Duke Snider).
We entertained other ragamuffin teams.
Bobby played short, I, first base
in pickup games in Brighton Beach,
deep in the heart of South Brooklyn.
We kept score, inaccurately.
We struck out often in the days
before younger baseball became so organized.
Those afternoons, dirty and hot,
birthed a life-long devotion to the game
where now an older man sits in front of the TV,
watches his team and remembers.
We were the Generals.

When Nelson Takes the Mound

When Nelson Figueroa,
my former student and present pitcher
takes the mound for the D-backs,
I will be twelve years old once more,
playing sandlot ball, on literally a sand lot.
Bobby Tzechtik will be at short,
and I will cover first base
for the Generals, the name we gave ourselves
in crayon on white tee-shirts
I took from my father's drawer.
Bobby and me were going to be major leaguers,
though I wore glasses and he was short.
Hey, if Nelson's dream came true, couldn't mine?
Couldn't I get the low throw from Bobby,
and cleanly scoop it up from the ground on one hop?
So when Nelson takes the mound again this spring,
me and Bobby will be right behind him,
slapping leather and screaming, "No batter! no batter!"

When Baseball Players Were Tough

Long ago in a baseball game far away
ballplayers were ballplayers,
who thought nothing of playing
both ends of a doubleheader.
Now, they split up doubleheaders
into day and night games to earn
double the admission gate.
Now, star ballplayers usually
sit out the second game.
Pitchers used to regularly go nine innings;
now, they are hardly allowed past six.
And, God forbid, the hurler breaks a nail,
he is immediately taken out of the game.
Give me the old-time players
who played with all kinds of injuries,
with nary a complaint, but a snarl.
There may be no cryin' in baseball,
but there sure is a lot of complainin'.
Toughen up, guys, and bite the bullet,
(or, at least, the bat handle.)
Be stoic, be brave, be fearless,
like your old, honored baseball brethren.

Who Remembers Herb Score?

The baseball gods giveth and taketh.
The Hall of Fame bears testimony to
players who have thrilled fans for years.
But, few, if any, remember Herb Score.
A lefty, with an incredible fastball,
he was compared to the legendary Bob Feller.
Chance dances on the air pushed back
by a 100 miles per hour heater.
Fortune smiles as capriciously
as a ground ball over a rough infield.
On May 7, 1957, Score was felled by
a line drive off the bat of Gil McDougald.
It hit him squarely in the eye, bloodying his face.
He was never the same afterwards.
How is it decided who should rise to the top
and who should literally fall by the wayside?
Ballplayers dream; baseball gods laugh.
When the cheering stops,
when the crowd has gone home,
there are few, if any people now
who remember Herb Score.

Why We Are Fans

In the film, "Fever Pitch,"
Jimmy Fallon's obsession with
his beloved Boston Red Sox
jeopardizes his relationship
with his girlfriend, Drew Barrymore.
Why are we such crazy fans?
Man, social by nature, needs a
House of Worship, secular or religious,
to demonstrate he is not alone
in an often alien and hostile world.
He needs to be connected to
something larger than himself,
to have a common goal that gives
a sense of community and purpose
at relatively little cost.
If your team wins, there is joy,
but if they are defeated,
nothing much of consequence is lost.
A winning team confirms one stands
with the champions, chest swelling with pride.
A losing team can simply be shrugged off.
Just wait until next year!

You Take It Too Personally

As with any good fan,
I live and die with
the undulating fortunes of my team.
When they win,
I am all smiles, at peace
with the positive harmonies of the Earth.
When they lose,
I wear an abject look of grief,
and feel catastrophe has been visited upon the world.
"You take it much too personally," my wife says.
How can I not when the future of my happiness,
or lack of it, rests in such precarious balance,
on the knife edge of wins or losses?
Each home run for my team elicits peals of joy,
while each home run for theirs sinks me
into the abyss of despair.
How delicate is my equilibrium
when it can be knocked off center
by the vagaries of hit and miss
by a group of men playing a boys' game?

2. Poems About Other Sports

There's More to Life Than Baseball

It would be myopic of me to believe
that baseball alone, while my favorite,
still rules the wide world of sports.
Many other games
vie for our attention,
proving that they, too,
have fans excited to
bring home championships.

Fandom starts early:
Barefoot African boys
kick around a soccer ball.
Young Italian men race
Ferraris on small-town tracks.
And in China many a teen
shoots arching 3's towards the net.

So, what follows now
is a small sampling
of other sports
beyond baseball,
all attesting to the variety
of humanity's passion for play.

Winter of My Discontent

Between football and baseball season
lies the winter of my discontent.
It's not that I hate basketball;
that isn't what I meant.
My TV has grown cold and dim.
There's nothing on the air,
just a few minor sports, perhaps,
or an occasional Olympic fare.
I do not know from ice-dancing,
I do not know from luge.
I have no interest in biathlons,
my depression's growing huge.
Oh, somewhere in this favored land,
the sun is shining bright.
Somewhere ballplayers are stretching,
preparing for the fight.
Somewhere hearts are happy,
the grass is always green,
But I sit here, sad and lonely,
with nothing on the screen.

Racing For Life

(In honor of Alex Zenardi)

It turns in a second, or a fraction thereof,
and I wonder who was watching out
for his safety that sun-blessed day.
Surely no one on the track, in the sky,
or in the grandstand that I could see.
No one prevented the crush and crash
of racing cars hugging each other on the turns.
One driver, Alex, cheated death, barely.
He could have cursed God; he didn't.
He could have given up; he didn't.
The miracle here was his resolve
to go on with his life, while others
might have been tempted to end it all.
He is now competitive again, a paracyclist,
hand-cranking the wheels in search of the flag,
proving what is destroyed, must be rebuilt,
what is lost, must be found again,
no matter if your life seems to go around in circles.

A George Carlin Basketball Poem

Some serious basketball questions:
I wonder why it is called a "foul" shot.
Does that mean it is inherently smelly,
and would drive players from the floor?
Would you say a "fair" shot should be launched
at least twenty feet from the basket?
And why is that center area called "top of the key"?
Do you need one to complete your shot?
I wonder, too, why they call the foul area "in the paint"?
Yes, I understand the hardwood might sport
a different color, but you're still on it, not in it.
It also bothers me that after four quarters
it's called "overtime," because everything
happens over time, doesn't it?
Shouldn't it be called "time over,"
because the final horn has sounded?
And finally, why is it still called a "backboard"
when most of the modern ones are made of glass?
These are some of my philosophical questions
as I sit here on the far end of the bench
where I play in the Y's over-40 league.

Air Jordan

It is reported that
Michael Jordan has made
$1.972 billion from
the sale of his signature shoes.
Hardly a footnote.
But what does that say about
American culture?
That we have no sole?
That we are laced with false values?
That shoes on our feet
are more important
than brains in our heads?
Bad puns mask the outrage.
You may say, if the shoe fits, wear it!
That's certainly a profitable business coda,
but also a hop, skip, and jump away
from the true problems of the land,
like the homeless, like the hungry,
who can't afford even one new Jordan shoe.
Consider this food for thought.

In the Dark

It gets dark here early on the East Coast,
Standard time, when the wind begins
to prowl around the neighborhood houses.
But, every evening in the failing light,
the teen-age boy next door
bounces a basketball on
the cement in his backyard.
There is no net, no backboard,
just the metronome sound
of the ball hitting the concrete.
But why?
Does he envision a career in the NBA?
No, I don't think so; he is no giant.
But I believe this external heartbeat
shows there will always be
a steady rhythm to his life,
a comforting, repetitive thwack
that will always be his assurance
that the world will be orderly
and peaceful in a world that is neither,
that the ball will always meet
his hand, providing and promising
certainty and security of
a future less turbulent and
unpredictable as the daily news
constantly makes up new rules.

D.J. Tucker

Working for minimum wage at McDonald's
certainly limits your horizons, giving
a faint view over the rim of an onion ring,
a glance through the slats of French fries.
I launch used cups like 3's into the trash cans.
Don't they know I'm gonna be a basketball star?
My manager's constantly on my case.
"You didn't clean up the tables.
You undercooked the burgers,
overcooked the chicken.
I'm gonna have to let you go, D.J.
You're really not cut out for retail."
No kiddin', man, I think.
That's OK, I'm gonna be an all-star.
Boss continues, "How slow you gotta be
if I hafta fire you from this place?"
"That's OK, man," I tell him.
"I'm gonna be an NBA highlight reel,
clean up in the paint, instead of
cleanin' up stupid tables,
run the fast break instead of wishin' for one,
ring up points instead of the stupid register.
Wait and see if I don't; I'm outta here."

Darius Mills

My boys say the only way outta the hood
is with a pass—a basketball pass.
My boys say the only way outta the hood
is with a jump—a jump shot.
My boys say the only way outta the hood
is with a high average—a points-per-game average.
Just because I'm Black and over six feet six
don't mean my life is defined
by the baselines of a basketball court,
that my worth is graded on how high I can leap,
and my future is measured by my variety of slam dunks.
I got a brain beyond basketball,
a heart beyond hoops,
but who will know or care about that?
Dudes look at me and say,
"Can he score in the paint?"
I got other dreams, guys,
even if I don't know what they are right now.

Joel's Father

He was 57 when he died,
living long enough to remember
the halcyon days of Knick glory,
when Dollar Bill and DeBusschere
ruled the courts, along with Clyde and Barnett,
and, of course, the captain, Willis Reed.
The ball whipped around the circle
like a flying bird, darting swiftly
from one post to another.
The father would bring his young son
to the Garden, tell him the stories
of the Knick five who were
the definition of teamwork.
He would tell him of the time
Willis walked out onto the floor
hobbling on his bum leg and
promptly sank his first two shots.
Joel never saw the old Knicks,
just had his father's words
locked into a vault in his head.
He promised himself one day
he would bring his own kids to the Garden,
and tell them the stories his father had told him.

An Homage to John Updike

Avenues Flatbush and R meet at right angles,
and on the corner you will see the Oasis Diner,
where Alan, tall and balding, waits the front tables.
Patrons hardly pay attention to him
as they order pancakes and other breakfast specials.
But I, sitting at the counter, remember.
Once he played for our high school team.
He was good, in fact, the best.
I saw him score 53 points in one home game,
a school record still.
His hands were like wild birds.
He never went to college, just waits tables,
and in his quick, skilled placement of knives and forks,
I see the elegant motion of a perfectly thrown bounce pass
that finds a cutting teammate on the way to the basket.
Off work, he goes back to his one-room apartment,
flips his baseball cap onto his old MVP trophy,
and searches the channels looking for the Lakers game.

The Mountaineer

At sea level, in the local Barnes and Noble,
the Indian man, slight, no more than 5'3"
was asked about the book he was carrying,
a volume with Mount Everest on the cover.
"Are you a mountaineer?"
asked a taller man on line behind him.
"Oh, most definitely," the shorter man said, proudly.
"Don't tell me you climbed that?" the other man joked,
pointing to the large coffee-table-size book.
"Not all the way to the top.
We were not trained to go above 23,000 feet.
For the summit you must train for six months.
I had not the time for that, maybe one day."
"My word, what do you see from 23,000 feet?"
"On a clear day you see the clouds below you,
and if you look up, you touch the hand of God."
The Indian man was then called by the cashier.
"Excuse me," he said, politely, paid for his book
and waved back. "Maybe one day you will climb."
The other man waved, too, paid for his book,
and went back to his sea level apartment,
thinking about all he had yet to accomplish.

Annie Roberts

My mother waitresses down at the diner,
the one between Pearl and Main.
My older sister got herself pregnant,
and lives with her boyfriend, the next town over.
I haven't seen my father in years,
and sometimes agree with that poem that says,
". . . life for me ain't been no crystal stair."
Listen, I ain't complainin' all that much.
I go to school, and help my mother out,
busing tables at breakfast at the diner
before I have to make my first period—gym.
My favorite activity there is the rock wall.
I am the fastest one up the side in my class.
The metaphor is too simple—I have to keep climbin',
no matter what obstacles are in my way.
I wish my life were as easy as "The Rock,"
that there would be some guarantee
I could make it over the top of the wall
and get outta this town for good.
Hah, please forgive me if I have to say,
I live between a rock and a hard place.

Martin Andrews

Cricket is my island's most popular sport.
Many were the days when I bowled on the pitch,
successful in my attempts to make the striker miss.
Then, like a tree uprooted, my dear parents
brought me here to the United States, where
most of my new contemporaries assumed
cricket was some kind of diminutive insect.
They laughed at me and my accent
when I spoke of wickets with balls and stumps.
They asked why cricket players always wear white.
When I explained that anything less would be heathen,
they could not contain their uproarious derision.
I, in turn, could not understand their strange game
of baseball with its home runs, double plays and errors.
I asked my dear mother when we could possibly go home,
and she told me, sadly, we are here for good, make the best of it.
I promised her I would try, but my soul still yearns
for those long, lazy afternoons when the tropical sun
in its radiance bounced off our awaiting bats
and sweat poured freely from our glistening brows.

A $600,000 Sack?

You got $600,000 for what? A sack?
Surely, a sack of rice or beans
isn't worth that much.
Oh, not that kind of sack.
A football sack?
You gotta be kidding me.
No, it's true—a defensive end
for the Jacksonville Jaguars
got a $600,000 bonus for
recording his eighth sack of the season.
What is wrong with this country?
Kids go hungry,
innocents get shot,
while government is gridlocked.
Yet a football player gets $600,000
for dumping a quarterback on his back?
Maybe I should get a bonus
for knocking a stranger to the ground,
and add some more money
if he doesn't get up.
What's the moral of the story?
Maybe I should have learned
how to tackle an opponent
instead of tackling my books.

A Father and His Son

My father took me
to Giants football games.
"Wait here," he'd tell me,
pointing to a space where
I had to stand while
he went and got the tickets.
(Today he would be brought up on
charges of reckless abandonment.)
We froze in five different stadiums.
I wanted to go home because
it was so cold and he'd
stuff another hot dog in me.
He never had much money,
but what he had, he spent on the Giants.
I did not understand the complexity of play.
"I want to go home," I said, fingers freezing.
"Here's the program; memorize the roster."
My father is gone now, over 40 years.
I wish I could still go with him to Giants Stadium.
I would not even complain about the cold.

Arco, Idaho

As the crow flies,
Arco, Idaho is equidistant
from Denver and Seattle.
It's a small farming community
with one main street.
Folks there are equally divided between
loyalty to the Broncos and Seahawks.
People will gather at the town's café
to watch the big game, eat and cheer.
How strange a country
when a football tossed for a bomb
draws more attention than planes
dropping bombs in a war.
How oddly obsessed a country we are
when the final score of a meaningless game
takes precedence over societal divisions.
Whether rich or poor,
together we watch the Super Bowl,
drink our beer, eat our chips,
and bet on the outcome,
setting aside, at least for the day,
the harsh realities of life.

On Thin Ice

My dad takes me to Minnesota Wild hockey games,
his attempt to cement father/daughter bonding.
He feels he has been shut out of my life
by my mother, the goalie, who protects me
like a tiger in front of the net.
"How's school?" he asks.
"School's good," I say,
thankfully followed by giant men crashing into the boards.
"You okay?" he asks.
"I'm okay," I say,
thankfully followed by the horn ending the period.
"I'll get some hot dogs. You want?" he asks.
"Okay, that sounds great," I say.
"You seeing someone these days?"
"Careful, Dad, you're skating on thin ice."
He groans and goes for refreshments.
In the last period the Wild score and win.
We slap high fives, but say nothing.
Our conversation, like a hockey puck,
just seems to skim the surface.

Amanda Berne

My parents' slippery marriage,
sliding slowly downhill towards divorce,
sometimes stops in mid-argument
when my father calls a winter truce.
He announces a family ski trip,
so that "we can all get to know each other,"
a ludicrous statement, one in which he sees no irony.
His money can't buy happiness,
but it sure can buy ski packages to exotic resorts
where hot chocolate and cozy fireplaces
delude us into thinking, for a few days at least,
our family, as fragile as hanging icicles, will survive.
My parents, feeling mellow at the inn,
talk about the old days when I was a baby, and
the future presented itself as unblemished as untrodden snow.
While they canoodle, I fly down the intermediate trails,
and then immediately turn around to take the lift up once again.
I come in for lunch, see them holding hands,
pivot, and leave for the mountain directly,
not wanting to disturb the delicate peace between them.
I smile, thinking it may all still hold together,
wishing it would snow all year 'round.

Penny Coles

You want to know what kind of week it's been?
My boyfriend left me for a tramp,
who is beneath him, literally.
My best friend borrowed $20 from me,
and gave it to her best friend.
My grades are so low at the community college,
I need a crane to lift them up.
My mother has filed for separation papers—from me!
And the apartment building where I live is so old
the rats collect Social Security,
But when I surf,
Ah, when I surf,
my real life slips under the water,
as I grip the top of the board
to float above my pain.

Juliette

She was always late for her lesson.
Her boss at the diner asked for an extra shift,
or she had to shop for a sick friend.
But her smile and lightness
easily dismissed any resentment he had.
Easy, too, to rearrange his tennis schedule.
She was studying English here in Brooklyn,
an exchange student from Paris,
who, when she missed a backhand,
smiled even wider and said, "Mais, Non!"
She moved with balletic grace,
floating above the lines.
"I must go back to the Sorbonne,"
she suddenly announced one session.
"I hope to back to the practice, no?"
making the tennis court seem
far heavier the next weekend.
He would wait for her however long,
patiently pounding forehands for his love.

Dark Tennis

I like the Eastern Europeans in dark glasses,
who claw and fight for every point.
Lose, and they will be sent back
to the goat hills of Transylvania.
Give me the competitor who challenges calls,
hurls his racket, and is generally unpleasant,
rather than the blond California boys,
who view their tennis as patrician play
before they become portly pros
at some exclusive tennis resort.
I prefer the player who digs in,
knowing he is short on natural talent,
but long on desire and heart.
Kudos to those contestants who consider
every double fault as a personal affront,
and who would gladly cough up a lung
reaching for a wide serve to the ad court.
Let me battle against the volley of death
with decidedly uncourtly manners
as I hit a screaming forehand
that just kisses the far baseline.

The Underdog

The term, coming from when they
held dog fights in the 19th century,
the winner was called "top dog,"
and the unfortunate loser
was labeled as the "underdog."
Today, the name is cuddlier.
We want to root for the underdog.
We want to be the underdog,
the person who has climbed up
from the bottom to reach the top.
Favorites are so boring.
Did anyone root for the Baltimore Colts,
or did we root for Joe Namath's Jets to win?
Did anyone root for the Baltimore Orioles,
or did we want the upstart Mets to win?
So today, when I watch the Super Bowl,
though I have no attachment to Ohio,
I will be rooting for a Bengals win,
just because they are called, "the underdogs."

About the Author

Mel Glenn has written numerous books of poetry about sports, religion, the state of society, and his Brooklyn neighborhood. He has also published 12 books for young adults, including *Jump Ball* (Dutton Books for Young Readers, 1997), *Split Image* (HarperTeen, 2002), and *Who Killed Mr. Chippendale?* (Puffin Books, 1999), which was nominated for the Edgar Allen Poe Mystery Award.

Mel retired from the New York City public school system in 2001, after teaching high school English for 34 years. He now devotes his time to writing, reading, and watching sports, while also teaching his fellow retirees about writing essays, fiction, memoirs, and poetry in classes hosted by his union, the United Federation of Teachers.

Mel lives in Brooklyn with his wife, Elyse, a retired elementary school teacher, devoted birdwatcher, and fellow world-traveler. One of his sons, Jonathan, is a television news executive, while the other, Andrew, is a technology whiz.

In early 2023, Mel was thrilled to welcome his first grandson, Casey, into the world. There is no truth to the rumor that he was named after the quintessential baseball poem, "Casey at the Bat." Two years later, Mel was just as exhilarated by the birth of his first granddaughter, Reese. She was born in the spring—just in time for baseball season.

www.ingramcontent.com/pod-product-compliance
Lightning Source LLC
Chambersburg PA
CBHW070936160426
43193CB00011B/1706